W9-BLN-354

Mount Rushmore

by Judith Jango-Cohen

PULL AHEAD BOOKS
American Symbols

Lerner Publications Company • Minneapolis

To my niece Carla, who has big dreams like Gutzon Borglum

Special thanks to Jim Popovich, Chief of Interpretation, Mount Rushmore National Memorial, for his enthusiastic assistance.

Text copyright © 2004 by Judith Jango-Cohen

All rights reserved. International copyright secured. No part of this book may be reproduced, stored in a retrieval system, or transmitted in any form or by any means—electronic, mechanical, photocopying, recording, or otherwise—without the prior written permission of Lerner Publishing Group, Inc., except for the inclusion of brief quotations in an acknowledged review.

This book is available in two editions:
Library binding by Lerner Publications Company, a division of Lerner Publishing Group, Inc.
Soft cover by First Avenue Editions, an imprint of Lerner Publishing Group, Inc.
241 First Avenue North
Minneapolis, MN 55401 U.S.A.

Website address: www.lernerbooks.com

Words in **bold type** are explained in a glossary on page 31.

Library of Congress Cataloging-in-Publication Data

Jango-Cohen, Judith.
    Mount Rushmore / by Judith Jango-Cohen.
      p.   cm. — (Pull ahead books)
    Includes index.
    Summary: Describes the meaning, history, and creation of the stone monument
to four American presidents carved into Mount Rushmore, South Dakota.
    ISBN-13: 978–0–8225–3801–1 (lib. bdg. : alk. paper)
    ISBN-10: 0–8225–3801–6 (lib. bdg. : alk. paper)
    ISBN-13: 978–0–8225–3755–7 (pbk. : alk. paper)
    ISBN-10: 0–8225–3755–9 (pbk. : alk. paper)
    1. Mount Rushmore National Memorial (S.D.)—Juvenile literature. [1. Mount
Rushmore National Memorial (S.D.) 2. National monuments.] I. Title. II. Series.
F657.R8J365 2004
730'.92—dc21   2003000384

Manufactured in the United States of America
4 – DP – 11/1/09

Whose giant face is this?

It is the face of **President** George Washington. His face is carved into Mount Rushmore in South Dakota. Four presidents are carved there.

The carvings of the presidents are a **symbol** of the United States. They stand for the country's first 150 years.

Gutzon Borglum had the idea for this
symbol. Many people in South Dakota
liked his idea.

So Gutzon looked for a tall, sunny mountain for his carving. His son Lincoln helped him. In 1925, they chose Mount Rushmore.

Gutzon decided to carve Washington.
He was the first U.S. president. Why
did Gutzon choose the others?

Thomas Jefferson added new land to the United States. This new land made the country twice as big.

Abraham Lincoln led the United States during the **Civil War**. The North and South fought each other. But Lincoln kept the country together.

Theodore Roosevelt had the Panama **Canal** built. This canal made it easy to sail from the east to the west.

Gutzon made a **model** of these four presidents. This model helped his workers make the giant carving.

Gutzon Borglum's Model
of Mt. Rushmore Memorial—
Washington, Jefferson
Roosevelt & Lincoln
—RISE STUDIO—©

In 1927, the carving of Mount Rushmore began. How do you think workers broke away the stone?

Workers blasted away giant blocks of rock with **dynamite**. The mountain rumbled with each dynamite blast.

14

Workers used **drills** to break away smaller chunks of stone.

Drillers worked high up on the mountain.
They worked in cages and in seats that
looked like swings.

Steel wires, called **cables**, held the workers on the mountain.

Gutzon Borglum watched over the workers. He also made safety rules.

Gutzon could not be at Mount
Rushmore all the time. His son took
over when Gutzon was gone.

Each night, dusty and tired men
plodded 760 steps down the mountain.

By 1936, workers rode up and down the mountain in a wooden cage.

Workers carved Washington first. In 1930, crowds cheered to see the first face on the mountain.

People came to see the carving of Jefferson in 1936. One year later, they cheered when Lincoln's face appeared.

In 1939, Theodore Roosevelt looked out from Mount Rushmore. By 1941, the last bits of work were done.

About 400 people worked on Mount Rushmore. They are listed at the mountain. Their grandchildren come to read their names.

Millions of people visit Mount Rushmore.
The mountain is a famous symbol.

Gutzon Borglum made this symbol to honor the United States. He hoped it would last as long as the mountain.

Facts about
Mount Rushmore

- The faces on Mount Rushmore are 60 feet high. That's about as tall as a five- or six-story building.

- Gutzon wanted to carve Jefferson on the end of the row of presidents. But the stone was not strong there. So Gutzon started over and carved Jefferson on the other side of Washington.

- Some drills weighed 80 pounds. That may be more than you weigh!

- Some workers were afraid of hanging over the edge of the mountain in the little cages and seats. At home at night, they had bad dreams and woke up hanging onto their beds. Gutzon gave these workers other jobs.

- Gutzon Borglum died on March 6, 1941, before his carving was done. His son Lincoln took over for him until the work was finished on October 31, 1941.

The Workers at Mount Rushmore

Most workers at Mount Rushmore had never carved stone. They were ranchers, loggers, or miners. On the mountain, they learned new jobs. Some built ladders or sharpened the cutting end of the drill, called the bit. Others placed the dynamite or hauled drillers up and down on cables.

Drillers were always coated with dirty, gritty rock dust. They had to scrub it from their clothes, hair, and skin. But they could not scrub off the dust they had breathed in. No one died from an accident while working on Mount Rushmore. But some died years later from breathing in the rock dust.

More about Mount Rushmore

Books

Adler, David. *A Picture Book of Thomas Jefferson.* New York: Holiday House, 1990.

Jackson, Garnet. *George Washington: Our First President.* New York: Scholastic, 2000.

Potts, Steve. *Theodore Roosevelt: A Photo-Illustrated Biography.* Mankato, MN: Bridgestone Books, 1996.

Turner, Ann. *Abe Lincoln Remembers.* New York: HarperCollins, 2001.

Websites

American Experience: Mount Rushmore
http:// www.pbs.org/wgbh/amex/rushmore

Mount Rushmore Information
http:// www.mountrushmoreinfo.com/

National Park Service: Mount Rushmore National Memorial
http:// www.nps.gov/moru/

Visiting Mount Rushmore

Mount Rushmore is located in the Black Hills National Forest near Keystone, South Dakota. Visitors can view it year-round.

Glossary

cables: strong wires made of twisted steel

canal: a waterway or path dug for water to flow through and boats to sail across

Civil War: a war between two groups of people in one country. In the 1860s, the people living in the North of the United States fought those living in the South.

drills: tools with a pointed end that can cut into stone and other hard things

dynamite: a special powder or material that can blow apart stone and other hard, strong things

model: a small copy of something

president: the leader of a country, such as the United States

symbol: an object that stands for an idea, a country, or a person

Index

Photo Acknowledgments

Photographs reproduced with permission from: National Park Service, pp. 3, 4, 16; © Joseph Sohm; Visions of America/ CORBIS, p. 5; Library of Congress, pp. 6, 8, 10, 11, 12; Rise Studio, pp. 7, 22; Independence National Historical Park, p. 9; © Underwood & Underwood/ CORBIS, pp. 13, 18, 21; Lincoln Borglum, pp. 14, 15, 24; South Dakota Historical Society-State Archives, p. 17; Bell Photo, pp. 19, 20, 23; © Judith Jango-Cohen, p. 25; © Lester Lefkowitz/CORBIS, p. 26; © Tom Nebbia/ CORBIS, p. 27; Verne's Photo Shop, p. 29.

Cover: © Joseph Sohm; Visions of America/CORBIS.